NORTH STAR

Also by L. S. Asekoff

DREAMS OF A WORK
(an Orchises book)

NORTH STAR

L. S. ASEKOFF

Orchises
Washington
1997

Library of Congress Cataloging-in-Publication Data

Asekoff, L. S. (Louis S.), 1939-
   North Star / L. S. Asekoff.
      p.   cm.
   ISBN 0-914061-57-7 (hardcover: alk. paper)
   I. Title
   PS3551.S334N67   1997
   811'.54—dc20   96-19975
                                        CIP

Grateful acknowledgement is made to the editors of the following magazines in which these poems first appeared: *American Poetry Review:* "Black Spring," "Black Suit," "Blue Flower," "Crowdoll," "Cygnus Olor," "Hangman," "Hôtel du Rêve," "In the Place of the Absence of Desire," "Invisible Hand," "Island," "Jubilee," "Last Call," "North Star," "Pilot," "Radio Soleil," "Rounding the Horn," "Sharktalk," "Starwork," "Swan," "The Master, 1941," "The Prisoner," "Tierra del Uomo," "Vigil," "Writing in the Rain;" *The Brooklyn Review:* "Loom;" *Field:* "Iceboats," "The Shoes Are Death;" *Pequod:* "Lily Photographed by Moonlight;" *Poetry:* "Flowers by the Sea," "In the House of the Deafman;" *Salamagundi:* "Yesenin;" *Sulfur:* "Reading after Dark."

"The Prisoner" was anthologized in *Articulations: Poetry about Illness and the Body* (University of Iowa Press 1994) edited by John Mukand. "Starwork" was reprinted by Inkspot Press for White Creek Press, Bennington, Vermont, 1993.

Manufactured in the United States of America
Published by Orchises Press
P.O. Box 20602
Alexandria
Virginia
22320-1602

G6E4C2A

For My First Readers

CONTENTS

i

ii

iii

iv

i

Starwork

If we are lucky
there will be time to imagine
how the dead might admire
this halo of cities but for now
we must follow the directions
one hand leaves for the other.
As in conversation sparks fly upward
so allegory takes wing against wreckage of night,
the swan song of a sun in its solitude.
In whose interest do they labor, we wonder,
these silhouettes of desire
cast back at us by the orphaned event?
& when no man remembers his mother or father
what can measure our loss—*techné*
as *telos*? At the vanishing point
where the mullah who fed his master's gold bird
gives way to the Sand Reckoner
sifting grains of light
lip service is paid to the names
once strange to us—problems of navigation
that leave us all in the dark.

Crowdoll

—*for Douglas Culhane*

To take the darkness in,
make friends with it,
lift up & out into the night
this limp broken wing
nailed to a melting shadow,
poor forked plaything
in blackface vanishing,
as though to say,
"After every why
a why-not." Risen
from fiery leaves,
the crowdoll's thin
smokesignals ask
forgiveness of
the keeper of stars
when a tree falls,
& you,
dark, anarchic, restless,
beholden only
to your own mind's
echoing, shapeless
shapeshifting *of* of "of" . . .

Loom
—for Paul Auster

So the wo/
man who

invented
the loom

invented
the lyre

impulse
domiciled

spinster
in the house of rime

Yet night
unweaves

what day
has woven

the starmap
fades

desire
a fiery branch in a stream

& now
the hour of the crows

Paul
how often have I

found myself
of late

lost
on familiar streets

after dark
& far from home

Frieze

Because it was cloudy   I copied off the wall
Broken blade   raised arm   bent knee &
In the distance   galloping away   two horses
It is not clear to whom they belong
Of what we know of them   it can be said
We know everything   yet everything
We know of them   is only a part of
What they knew   & remember   unlike us
These passionate sufferers cannot act
The man I loved   I idolized totally
Gritted my teeth   & went through hell for him
Then the paint started to peel   perhaps I do have
A black streak in me   still each day brings new flowers
Into the house of the dead   through a double-pane
The reservoir's icy light   shadow of gingko
Shaken by no wind   & the semi-transparency
Of my own fingers   passing through them
A red oil truck   Mystic Transport   uncoils its hose
Into a snowbank where   a man in yellow slicker
Loiters   the frosted stem   glassy goblet
Of his breath   shatter against the dark
Clairvoyance of this air

Iceboats

Out of such icy darkness
who has called them?
Shadow flowers,
white kings,
citadels of breath
chiseled on a pane
by that quick gentle killing thing—
the frost's chill fire.

Pale endeavors
of our wannest henchmen,
elbow of nothing,
Gloucestor's pearls,
life's frozen decrescendo—a white pitcher
pouring forever
into a porcelain bowl.

Listen,
the king's singers are ruled by fear
yet the melody lingers
like illness or
a white telephone
in a white room blankly ringing, ringing . . .

Look,
how isolate
& bravely now
through the keyhole of time they sail
the oblique light
of their vanishing—iceboats at dawn,
shadows swanned on snow.

The Shoes Are Death

Dim dimming dimmer
A blind man follows stepping stones
To a place where the ghost of categories rests
Beneath its cloak of many colors

This is the branching way
World in a backward look
Here the furious trees
Shake their fists at the stars
& all the words are named after somebody's mother

Yet the artifice ends in not knowing when
To stop to go on
You stop you go on again
Azure . . . measure . . . beige . . . garage . . .

The discernible difference is less
Than the wavering shade
On the porch of evening fades
From the grasp of one in whose debt we are left
Although he is deaf to it

Jubilee

Here is a lazy miracle of light,
a blind man picking snowpeas under the July moon.
Strung lyre, lustrous climbing vine, luminous luminous mind.

Inching slowly
over the lowlying kingdoms of the quick & the dead
what we touch we feel, & what we feel we taste & eat.

My friend,
we have followed the Drinking Gourd north,
fired our revolvers at the sun.
We are living in the slipstream of another's pain.

Soon we shall wake from a century's sleep
like the fabled waterlily,
Victoria Regina,
out of whose waxy whiteness springs all & everything—
the enormous flowering into *nowness*.

Annunciation

"I love the way light travels
in a stone house, lemons
wintering on a sill, chill music
the wind makes as the river drains
to salt marshes, a flowering stain.
We are well." On the other side,
Guido's black wall, gold branches,
& the Virgin, a blue candle, waiting
for the luminous dove of division
to descend. *O, dubiossi
disiri.* I close my eyes,
for a split second lost inside
the silhouette of that desire—
a crazy sensual light
like fire over ice fuses you
in flight—twin sisters wild
with schoolgirl crushes
practicing on featherbeds after dark
all the dangerously delicious
secret swooning kisses
kept from boys—shadow swans
by flashlight—rising, rising to
the black moon within you, & I,
who can give you everything but
the one thing—fearing
the world on fire—pick up my pen
to write you out of Eros & out of anger . . .

Joy

When you showed me the yellow bowl
fired with raku glaze

it seemed too somber somehow
for a child of fourteen to have made.

As you lifted it to the light
I could feel the growing desire

coming through you in flashes
to smash it—shatter

that fragile beauty,
the pleasure it gave me.

Sharktalk

Pricked by the North star's spur
all night our lovelocked bodies urged
the heartless muscles on
further than they could go
until as bleakly blue day broke
hand-in-glove
we breathless grasped
la petite mort—your forked ecstasy, choked cry,
my sea urchin,
a lost child sobbing for her father.
Coming apart, we open our eyes,
glazed, evasive, narcotized.

Now,
as though the lips of the wound
cried out for the knife,
sharktalk begins . . .
Clouded by brute anger
we strike for the mark, blindly true,
in broil of blood
trading cruel hurt for hurt
with that bitter charity
only intimate strangers show.
Each wanting what the other cannot give,
on this hard bed, we,
unforgiving, lie—live, let live.

As you pack for the North country's
white-capped peaks, darkly scattered lakes,
islanded in nightlight glow
I, disconnected, float . . .

Distantly, I feel the first quavering note
& secret surging joy of one about to come
into the kingdom of himself,
see as by razor gleam
suspended in water
a body,
slowly unraveling crimson ropes,
pale shapes circling the edge of sleep.
Hissing like dry ice,
they whisper all I know & fear & fear to know.

Muntzer

Losing kingdom after kingdom
we waded up to our bridles in blood
the riotous field. I woke from my dream
crying, *Let the perfumed dove tremble*
under the sickle moon &
the brant fox bark at false dawn
of these fires. The living God
is sharpening his scythe in me
so later I may cut down the red poppies
& blue cornflowers! Iron striking fire
from iron, hidden engines drive the shadow
out of the gated city of desire
& darkness takes flight—a sooty wing
speckled by stars. In its beak—bloodmeat,
a savage sunset smeared on a mirror.
& below, these women,
massive backs bent to the stony flow,
sing as they rinse night-soiled sheets.

Yom Kippur Poem
—for Sholem Aleichem

When the tailor with ashen eyes
smiles at you & says, *Son,*
this coat will last you a lifetime.
In fact, they way you look
maybe two lifetimes,
do not lament the luck
which is no luck.
My Friend, it is better
to hold a candle to the sun
than lie down in darkness
with the seller of dreams.
Today you shall stand
among the elders of Nightingale *shul*
in your father's black hat
& gold-braided shawl to ask,
Why is the goat more honored than Isaac?
Is Rabbi Akiba blind in heaven?

Radio Soleil

I sat on the porch waiting for my earthly father.
After the night of despair,
the mourning of good intentions.
I was fighting for the life of my right hand.
Slowly the numbers circled the clock.
A flinty hoof pawed the ashes.
Inside the saltbox I could hear the winter bees.
Below the swell & throb,
a thundery undertow,
moonboots shattering frozen light,
while a microtone away
the snowy bough of an evergreen swayed
to the counterweight of a crow.
At the end of Wing Road,
where the mystic chiropractor
mixes breath & bone,
white windows showed
a fire inspector dancing with a red dwarf.
The man with one hand urinated.
Flames splashed all over the wall.
My Golden Eagle #2 sang:
Command like the wolf,
obey like the lamb.
Slow oysters,
sudden pearls.
Fear knows no friend.
You have the good fortune
to be dealing with the dead.
The Sun network flashed its black cascade—
the Bay Psalter's
Venetian L,

night lightning, influenza,
streams of stars,
the astrodome of a cell.
Among the flickering shards I saw
wind-iced wings,
darkly pale & signaling:
Null/One Null/One Null/One
Pray for the owl of Sarajevo.
The three sisters of Kafka.
Look to the heavens but
mind your shoes.
They are dying in paradise.

Fire Queen

You are tired of being the fireman's wife,
ironing for the Rat Man & the Latin master.
Each night shrimp boats go out under the stars,
waiting for the capsules to descend.
As firewater is to the Indian, you say,
so are dreams to me. Still, you believe as we do
there are invisible forces in the universe,
evidence of things unseen. Step out the door,
distant points gleam back at you—forceps, stirrups, a . . .
Light floods the fontanelle!
Through the watery veil the sun burns like a bride.
Adrift in the red shift, fished out of the blue,
a flotilla of small lucite boxes
& curled inside like prawns on ice, the unborn,
soles pointed toward the polestar.
My beautiful TV babies! you cry.

Mister Honeyblue, maybe some day
I'll give up my dreams of the moon & the stars,
marry a fat man, learn to praise
the grey days of heaven, braid gold brooms
to sweep the cinders away.
For now I sit here connecting the dots,
taking pictures of the snow.

NIX HOPE IN X
the telegram read
DALMATION POST
MODERNIST DOG OF
MOMENT & was signed
SPARKS THE RADIOMAN

All night you heard the boxes humming in the dark.
Remember your mission, the voice said.
I am a Universal Donor, type-O, you replied,
& willing to give if only you ask me.
Evening grey. Morning red, said the voice.
Someone is dying, you cried. *Someone is dead.*
Here are the time-sick, sick of time, the voice said.
Spinning in space, a glass of Tang on a tray.
Take this grey pill for morning terrors & zero-g,
this little pink one for grief.
Pity the astronaut's mother, you said,
who floats on the gentle swells of the sea.
The higher you rise, the further you fall, the voice said.

That black & blue mark?
Pinch of Old Lobster Claw,
McCoy, the oilman, who worships me.
Called back from a pool hall in Hell,
he blocks the sun's rays.
I see the silver razor of the moon,
the chalked tip of his cue,
a diamond sparkler big as a pig's knuckle.
He wraps me in a gold chemise
stitched with a swarm of Italian bees.
Baby, I'm a travelin' man
who got a lion in his mouth.
Let me take you downtown for lunch,
shove my love-candle in your cake,
light the fuse!
Honey, let me smoke your hive!

At the Phoenix Firehouse,
the firemen are playing Night Baseball,
3's, 9's, Queen of Diamonds wild.

Through the blue haze of smoke,
bright pixels flicker,
matchsticks spill across the screen.
You see the axe, the hose, the gold pole,
the red machines gunned in chrome.
Swirling across the dark sky of Scorpio,
the flowing tail & mane of a runaway galaxy,
The Horse in a Whirlpool,
at its spiralling eye
a black microdot on which is inscribed
The Fireman's Code:
DO NOT MAKE LIGHT OF HOLY THINGS!

Mister Honeyblue, who am I?
The white ewe with a red dress on?
A blind lady leading dalmations through the snow?
Damnation's salvation? An underground star?
Now here now there nowhere at all,
I'm scat & scatter to the cat who scans—
peep-hole photon, striptease of light,
a golden event in a black box!

Put one hand on your pain, the voice says,
the other on the ray-dee-oh!
Here is a boat for the poor to sail in!
Here is the tool nobody has!
Here the aubergine glove of your lover, the boxer, swerving
among shadows,
a blue towel for smothering the black light of starlings, smoky
lamp of owls!
Here is a shimmering gold chemise stitched with a swarm of
Italian bees!
Here is the lion dreaming on its throne!

Soon you will hear his boots thundering up the stairs,
who carries the axe & the hose,
brings babies out of burning buildings,
scatters ashes on the roses you watered.

My kingfishers & morning glories,
my black hollyhocks, albino crows,
my silver boombox & licorice stick,
my Mystic Knights of the Golden Lodge of the Sea,
my White Night Watchers of Bethel & Salem,
my Holy Rollers coming in,
your EUOSSA EUOSSA USE your REBA SERA CALA NALA
your KAMA LEULLAH SAYE SALAH your AGLE LAGLE
LAGLE LAGLE
your SAH RAH EL ME SAH RAH EL ME
your ENE MENE MO

I see the fire, see the sky,
the rivers & bridges burning, burning,
the ladders of ice, the fiery pole,
the engines glowing in red & in chrome,
the white gladiolas of his eyes!

Fish, fish
A BLACK LION HAS SWALLOWED THE SUN!
where does the water begin?

ii

North Star

You are facing the harbor & the open sea.
Behind you, smoldering ruins, the iron city.
Across fragrant waters, the country of forgotten names.
You are travelling light, carrying nothing with you
but what you have lost. Tomorrow, you have been told to bring
only herbs & spices—almond, vanilla, sage, rosemary, rue.
I guess you could say you are doing as well
as can be expected. Cell by cell,
your hands are beginning to forget the feel of her flesh—
her neck, her breasts, her thighs. You are cured,
almost cured. Day by day, the language you speak has become
a barbarous mockery of your mother tongue.
Only this morning you woke to the familiar smell
of a tiny blue flower you no longer know the name of.
Still, you are fearful of calling too early
& hearing it ring & ring & ring . . . & thinking . . . & then
beginning to think . . . Just yesterday, you walked into the gloom
& lit a candle in her name & made a wish,
a wish for her. What kind of wish you will not say.

So, you are in the belly of the beast. Stormy
weather. You have reefed your sails
& are riding it out, scooping water with a net.
As wave after wave sweeps over you,
the old nausea returns—an underground cloud,
black wing. Overhead, amber waters close,
darkly gold as a toad's eyelid. When you stare at your hands,
how distant they seem from you. Look in the mirror,
what do you see? Your oldest friend,
truest enemy. *To slay the monster,*
a voice says, *you must first find him.*

After death, comes forgiveness. (In moonsilver darkness
she slides from room to room, silent & voluptuous
as a wolf.) *Where there is lawful terror,* you cry,
the stars are claws! Then you pull the red thread,
& everything unravels in your hands . . .

                                              Shuddering,
you wake to the throb & thrum of water & screw.
Churning like an oiled swan,
the *North Star* turns from the harbor
& breasting the waves, steams for the open sea.
In the thrilling clarity of a new freedom
you see everything as though for the first time—
the red axe bolted to the wall, lifeboats lashed to the deck,
the captain astride the bridge, wild-eyed & drunk on vodka,
steering into the stinging salt spray.
The strong current swiftly unfolds bolts of luminous blue.
Pearly grey clouds float overhead—light tenders in a sea of oil.
Beside you, she stirs—all white & gold.
With a free hand you stroke her long, lovely neck.
Smiling under the sun's blade she whispers,
Darling, you will be my avenger!

Pilot

When the man with the star comes to get you,
he can't find you here. You're on water, Son, & water's
no legal address. Myself, I was born on the river. I loved God,
& I loved the river. I didn't question it, I accepted it,
its rules & its currents, & it took me—a child of nothing,
& made me a child of the river. Before I went into the world
what I knew—the seed—took root, grew & flowered.
The river was my Book of Knowledge, but they knocked me
   down.
Same man put barbed wire 'round a mountain sold the river.
No one owns a mountain or a river, lest it's Indians, maybe,
or the people. When Waldo Emerson bailed his pal, Henry
   Thoreau,
from Concord jail for vagrancy on the Post Road,
Congress earned their double-eagle daily reporting to
Sergeant-at-Arms, & they kept a dungeon for goldbrickers
in the Capital cellar. Nowadays, what makes them tick?
   Greed
& dirty politics. Once, in Baton Rouge, I had a drink with the
   late
Air Secretary. "Sir," I said, "you ruled the roost. How come
you let them foul our nest?" & he leaned over, tapped my chest,
"Gotta make a living, don't I?" Leastwise, he was honest.
& that was years before the chain of evidence led us from
all the loyal slaves of Watergate to the Pharaoh in the White
   House
with the smoking gun. Oh, it's all yellow silk. Pole to pole, the
   rich
whisper to the rich. Bismarck's banker's still in business. Son,
I always say we Americans may be ignorant, but we ain't
stupid. I can make my own projections. Climb a hill, halfway

I know the incline, rate of speed. Give me manifestoes,
bills of lading any ship this harbor—red Georgia ore,
'bama cotton, Kansas wheat, cold-rolled steel from Illinois
or Tennessee, shiny tin Toyotas in a row—I'll tell you where
       we'll be
seven years from Sunday. Just last week out these waters
I fished a perch—eyeballs purblind baby moons. Son, this
       river's
not Big Muddy anymore. It's a sewer, pure & simple—polluted
from St. Paul to Cairo, Memphis, Gulf of Mexico. What's this
       country
coming to? I believe, as the Good Book says, Jesus walked upon
       the waves,
Moses parted the Red Sea. We sit on our decks at sunset,
drinking beer, piss downstream, & call it freedom. Mark Twain
may have been a habitual masturbator & a proven liar but
he was dead right about one thing when he swore
if we don't mend our ways & learn to care
some day soon we'll end up windfarming in Nebraska
or crash in darkness plumb into the sun.

Under the Star

Father's theatre was the most beautiful in Berlin,
three balconies, all red mahogany,
under gold eaves, higher than heaven.
From the wings I saw shadows swoop & fall,
tangled in a net of light.
Father was the smartest man I knew.
Little one, he said, *you must learn to do*
what no one can take from you.
Every day after school I followed the fingers of Ella—
needle, thimble, thread—
Pay attention, she said,
The hummingbird drinks from the blue flower.
It is like dancing with God.
I guess you could say I was born
under a lucky star. My first birthday telegram
came from Piscator, once I wore
Meyerhold's hat, the silverfoil ring
from Brecht's cigar.
When I was eleven, I sewed Joan Dark's gown.

Soon, soon, the black thread
was woven into the gold. We
were the chosen people. Under the star,
Mother was sent to Buchenwald, Grandmother & I
to the camp at Gurs. & Father? Dear Father?
One day a man came on donkey to Gurs
& took me away. We rode all night,
slept in a tree, next morning
crossed a river, entered a city.
Dogs barked—a gate opened—a door.
Out the dark, a voice whispered, *My child,*

I am Sister Maria Theresa.
I knelt to kiss the hem of her gown.

The rest is history—the dark aria . . .
I have heard the voices, listened
to the names, lifted the mask to see
what is hidden from us only
by what we are . . . Even now,
as the last light breaks in waves
over Buenos Aires, & the hummingbird drinks
from the blue cup of evening,
I follow the unwinding river of thread
as though it were the single sentence
of this miracle—my life. Just last week
the Queen of Netherlands sent me
a dozen tulips from the House of Orange,
& this is the dress of the Generalissimo's wife,
the silk cape of the mad ventriloquist, her lover.

Hangman

My wife's garden was a paradise of flowers.
All the prisoners loved it.
Gold trumpet of daffodils, lilies' white fire,
antediluvian blue of morning glories opening on the vine,
& those glowing black lions, the sunflowers, their beards of
     bees.
The promise of bulbs in the cellar got us through winter.
During lengthening twilight, sheepgut vibrated from the harp
     in my hands.
Sometimes, late at night, when the whole earth seemed to me
a vast altar upon which is sacrificed all that is living,
I would seek relief in the stable among my beloved animals.
Mounting my horse, I would whip him round & round the ring
trying to get the terrible pictures out of my head.
I was ashamed of my uniform.
                              One evening, I stood at the gate
watching our servant girl fold laundry from the line
when a voice in the wind called out my name.
I looked up. No one was there. Yet I had heard it, clearly,
     distinctly—a woman's voice,
soft, undulant, haunting, diaphonous almost, the sheerest
     fabric
shaken by the wind, & a shiver went through me
as when blood calls to blood its blue tattoo.
It was the hour between the dog & the wolf. Light trembled . . .
The great bell of heaven dipped & swelled.
Beyond the compass of the swallow's wing
I could see slowly unraveling ropes of smoke,
the silver quiver of poplars beside the tracks,
& the words came to me, *"A dying man hammers the wings of
     angels,"*

& I was for a moment lost & afraid.

                                           Icy tingling
rippled through me, the chill penumbra of, how say it,
      unfeeling's feeling,
as though there flowed through phantom fingers
a skein of shocked silk like woven water,
a stocking of skin stripped from the bone,
& a dark caul fell over me & I dropped into bottomless
      darkness,
darkness of night without measure, night without end,
night with its mud & its *merde,* hiss of gasses, howls of terror,
      cries of pain,
night with its crackling black fires & river of worms,
night where no one is more sinned against than the unborn, the
      forgotten,
where no brother buries his brother in the ashes & cinders of
      the field,
& the victor, sharpening his sword, strikes stars from stones.

The Prisoner
—for Amnesty International

Bowing before boot & fist
you learn to hide

small hands in sleep
& flee in terror like a child

from the pain that makes you
human. Soon hour of the

"blue lit stage" when
you will open like a rose

before blind operators
& their machines—"a telephone."

It will be a birthday party
with tea & burnt toast

where you will star—stranger
holding the heavy stone,

tarantula rattling
bamboo bars—each betraying

scream gagged by shit
in a paper bag. Left you

will be these little
miracles—*corragio*

in a matchbox, a song
carried faintly on the wind,

scent of periwinkles &
black drink of oblivion.

Rounding the Horn

I was a week away from the red chip when they outed me from
     Gay AA
for phonesex in the detox closet, swilling bottles of phony
     cologne—*Esprit*,
bootlegged by my bunkmate, a walleyed cowboy from Melville,
     Long Island.
Brothers, Sisters, I said, cursed from birth with a terrible thirst
     by the Dreaded Enabler
who bent my elbow at the Brazen Head bar, nursed bitter milk
     from barrels at Baileys,
I was born of a triple-Virgo by the blind porter at World's End,
the black Irish Jewish Catholic alcoholic offspring of
that lost tribe of penmen, those heinous sheenies & Arab
     seamen, Shawn & Shem.
Or, as they say in Mayo, to make a short story malinger, Once I
     drank to stop the voices,
now I drink to bring them back. At which point Schein turned to
     Schauer with a sour grin,
Dollink, tell me, vy iz Cleo's noze zo long? Becawz, my deeah,
     she'z de qveen ov de Nial!

Locked on the mountaintop with all the 12-steppers & those
     jovial overweight
Franciscan friars whose strict diet condemns them to die at 50 of
     beer & potatoes,
I was sore all over as though fallen from a great height
with a hollow ache in the blades at my back where the wings
     once were.
Kneeling before the porcelain bowl I saw a ghost-face flower
     haloed by my fiery orange hair

& someone had lipsticked across the glass roof of Hell: NO
 BUDY LUVS NO ONE.
That's when the statues started talking back to me . . .

Grand Rounds. Doctor Glanders illuminates a map of the dark
 side of the moon—
its rilles & furrows & lunar seas. Weighing each word on his
 tongue like a turd on a golden scale,
he points toward me. This lad has the brain of an 80 year old
 man!
With all due respect, I reply, you are not addressing some
 riverboat queen
with a taste for pink magnolias & scarlet cock. See the pearl in
 this left ear?
I got it rounding the Horn in rough trade, foul weather, lashed
 to the mast,
loony as a snowbird, wailing, wailing like Ma Rainey for all
 those the black ox has taken away—
the little grey lady on the subway, the red Indian of the sun.
In sum, my dear externs & interns, I may be a refugee from a 3rd
 world country
recuperating in your 4th world now, but when I recover I'm off to
 the 5th!

Well, I was high as a winged-horse on astrograss & singing
 Hosannas
when they wheeled me, the sweet dove-grey Sisters of Bilitis,
down white-tiled tunnels to the house of icy waters & electric
 beds—Auschwitz for angels!
Honey, one crooned, as she strapped me in, just how many years
 do you really want?
Tapdancing between powerpoles in my metal skullcap & iron
 shoes

I heard death rattle in a baby's fist, then the juice jolted
   through me &
I'm riding the 3rd rail from Zeroville toward Ringsend—the
   Alpha Express!
Blue movie of windows brings me to a cindery river, switching
   stations, rosebrick gardens,
Sunnyside, Queens. Through cloudy curtains I see my own
   mammy, toothless, dying
in the bed I was born in. Who is that holding her in his arms?

Cap'n McCall, Sergeant Malarky, my brave night crawlers,
   wave mechanics,
after the last go-round, how will it end? Bible? Bottle? Gun?
   Breathers Anonymous?
A nanosecond of spark, then out in the dark again, in my moth-
   hole overcoat
under a starless sky? There's a chill in the air, but I know the
   way—a step at a time.
Hedgerow. Blackthorn. Elm. At the end of the lane, purple
   shadows, a faint afterglow.
Thatched roof. Plume of smoke. & the white horse standing at
   the gate, still as a stone.

Last Call

*"Only those who are truly naked
can enter the Kingdom of Feeling."*
EDWARD DAHLBERG

You feed the sheep each morning.
At night you count them.

You sit by the window
in your borrowed clothes

Quietly drinking
as the white statues rise against the sky.

How will it end?
This hole to nowhere?

O, you are calm & collected
as a fist

& clever, clever
in your shrewd repose.

You know Hell inside out.
The room with no clocks & a door

& the wee little key
shining shining in your pocket.

Opening the blacked-out daybook
you write

With the Roman calm
of a man dotting i's in a suicide note

We're all mates on a westward ship.
We have not yet drunk to the darkest dawn.

iii

Invisible Hand

Perhaps there has never before been such an open sea,
the malady of death & the long affair
in the absence of history.
Because we love the things we lose,
we are tempted by the cynic's dogma—
a lantern in a briar bush,
the monstrous fish with the human face.
& there are close calls.
As the ferryboat slides from the slip,
the unborn whisper to the dead.
"La via' del tren subterraneo es peligrosa."
"I was held on Angel Island waiting for my witnesses to
    appear."
"The women's umbrellas protect us from strange suns."
Let the Evangel open the Book of Numbers,
the poor man count his sheep,
sequela . . . septentrion . . . phalaros . . . ,
the delirious plowing of this sea leads us to
"the merchant who sailed to Constantinople,"
"the woman who sold three pearls,"
the pursuit of the eversame in the name of the new,
the sins of the fathers outliving their sons.
& what furrows our wake? Mere wind & spray?
A seahorse exploding into a star?
The pale cataclysm with fins?
The trapdoor springs to the lucid nightmare.
Entering the city, we give up the sky.
Here is the dawn of the bearded men,
water drinkers in smoky cafes
where slender fingers twist wire & crepe for funerals of spring
& the lamplighter is an underworld informant.

"My brothers,
in the ruined palace where poison is a sacrament
the great ones spend thirty years in chains
dreaming of the sun
while we are blackmailed by the theatre of white telephones
& jailed for the song of small flowers.
Now the red radio brings news of the dead.
Give us back our names! they cry.
Must we sail forever under this dark sky?
What was our crime?
A taste for chocolate?
The bittersweet oranges of Palestine?
As the cave billows with shadows & smoke,
we see the children, heads on fire,
a deaf alphabet signing away—hostages to futurity.

In the House of the Deafman

Turning your back on the past,
its causeless chains of causation,
horses of the sea driven under the moon's mad eye,
you live for the moment free of illusion,
Goya, after the revolution,
returning, hopes dashed, to the rubble of Madrid,
the stone house of the deafman.
Slowly you are reduced to cruel outlines, cartoons,
the brutal palette of the final years—blacks, greys
with just a splash of red. & yet, tonight,
as voices in the next room describe the unseen mountain
you are surprised by the luminous cloud
of a new feeling, the modern nostalgia
for what drifts toward us across the abyss,
a futureless future . . .

Crossroads

The man who offers a ticket to the future
has one hundred percent disability
& no visible wounds.
Truly anger buzzes inside him
like a bee inside a brown bottle
& when a match flares across the night of his eyes
roses blaze in Addis-Ababa.
Although he proclaims himself "a lifetime democrat"
you still see the old believer in the new man
who heard just in time
a hammerblow strike the first statue down.
Like us he has learned to speak ill of the dead
with crossed fingers & in whispers only
for the old gods have a way of rising again—
laughter of the earth
bubbling beneath the city's eggshell tar
its terra-cotta towers marble stelae.

Yesenin
(Hotel d'Angleterre,
St. Petersburg, 1925)

Interned by the weather
& the infinite prison of reflection
a black man in top hat & tails
nurses the monocled moon in a shot glass.

Take off your gloves.
Undo the apricot silk loveknot.
Dip your pen into a sunrise of horses slaughtered on snow.

Flaming gold cupolas,
old believers cry, *"Comrades, awake!*
Dreams are products of the workers' sleep!"
Kulaks in muddy boots drive their tractors over graveyards of
the sky.

Iconoclast of the future chained to Adam & the dynamo,
oriole of that brief dawn,
shameless & sincere you sacrificed your song
for the revolution on wheels—
Winged Victory crushed by a locomotive.

What can we say of you?
Like us, seeing the better, you followed the worse;
your words—a fishbone stuck in the throat of the State.

Free at last
from the indifferent turning of the earth,
you swing, a clapperless bell, above
our hollow oracles, history's echoing chasm . . .

Farewell, my friend.
Under the measureless shadow of the white raven wing
years roll by like boxcars toward the starved heart of winter.

Flowers by the Sea
—for Fairfield Porter

Nothing is arranged here, each artlessly
displayed in uncomplicated light—stippled
pinks, violets, lavenders, sprightly
yellow sprays—all painted on air
luminous as the day Giotto drew
his circle round the sun. Yet sea-dappled
surfaces, the flowering verge
hint at solemn pleasures, intimate
mysteries beyond the humdrum. Only later,
looking back through screened familiar places
we feel more sentimental about than
people, do we discover wavering
in heat-haze veiled transparencies,
ghosts of no-color, nameless ones
who will not come when we call them home.

Lily Photographed by Moonlight, 1863

At the time it must have seemed
a bold experiment in a new way of seeing,
the gorgon-eye that stopped
the locomotive in its tracks freezing
against fall of night
the unfurling transparency
of this lily—white magic trapped
in a black box. What langorous anxiety they felt
catching nature in the act
we late arrivals cannot know, yet
we imagine how she, shifting, under the moon's
quicksilver spill, her shadowy
repose, petal
by pale petal unfolds
to better drink the darkness in,
& he, feigning chill indifference, the lens
between them, keeps his necessary
distance, slowly exposing
the glass plate. To our impatient eye
such long looks, loving delays of light
seem luxuries of an earlier,
surer world, innocent
as our first parents—deferrals
of pleasure in the nightfall faith
there will always be time enough to take
the walk, long-planned,
beside a glacial mountain lake, blue with lupins.

Hôtel du Soleil

—for Michael Palmer

Between floral excess & this crazy wisdom
is a language like fresh paint slapped on old wood,
"the slow splash of a flower."

As the gold pencil sails under your arm
a lonely mime in the next room imitates
owls making love to porcupines.

Here to think of nothing is to think of the song
the rocks dream of as the machine stops
& we all go into the deep house

where what is given to us is what is taken back—
radiolaria, starfish, snowflake,
the light that breaks from homesick sailor's eyes.

How robustly he strides over the hill
in his broadbrimmed black hat,
whose lamp is the world's shadow.

"Drink the fire," he says, "for the night is falling.
The face on the surface erases no other."

Reading after Dark

Nothing ages as rapidly as the new
branching fields of weather & the economy—
the pure series of interruptions
coined by accidental light—sooty illuminations
in a cloud; smoky bullion; the mellow glow
photographed off old stones in courtyards; honeyed hive
of morning sun; a dreamy pee in the snow
as drowsiness overtakes you—hiss
of ice steaming, gold hole you sink into.
Finally, it is a matter of "light house keeping,"
knowing how to or not to do, emerging as the right
to remain invisible—hidden entrance
to the royal theme: the Golden Book
where you first saw the black spell of letters
broken—Dora's adorable bees or mere ardor's
mirroir d'or—angel at the guillotine.
Perhaps we are too easily pleased by this journey
nobody goes on—its dangerous windows, dumb
impediments, fallen walls, &—the geometer's
nightmare—monstrous torsoes
carved from silence & from time, all the politics
of mapmaking as the low hills rise in waves
to meet us & mountains knock us smack in the eye.
Yes, travelers should only read after dark,
but when the floods come, *Signore*, all the shit
rises to the surface, giving off the stench
of a language (scented with whorish green
Spanish soap) that smells as we do.
Under the smoking lamp, you labored—old rough
skin redskin pig sprouting wings—producing sentences
sublime in their foreshadowing, past

as premonition, just catching up to us—the late dark lyrics
dusting with first light a bowl of blue Sicilian lilies.

The Master, 1941

If there are legends in life, this
is one of them: snowflakes fall
on painted mountains—fiery lakes, crystal stars,
& so he discovers in the laboratory of nature
the controlled accident of art.
Far from rootless multitudes of Paris & Berlin,
"the modern bacillus"—Jews,
he chooses clarity & solitude,
chill North light, takes as his name
the town he was born in—*Nolde*, the peasant.
Fascinated by flowers & their fate,
plants with his wife Frisia's first garden,
bows at height of noon in his white beard to kiss
the burning chalice of the poppy.
Evenings, walks the lowland's glowering
orange thunderheads, gold-thatched roofs,
black windmills, fields of flax.
As the immense red face of the sun,
an angry farmer, hissing, sinks
into the green wave's mountainous depths
a giant hand grasps his. *"Brother-in-blood,"* voices cry
& the heart of creation beats for all.
Loyal even now in his disloyalty,
he draws the shades, prepares before him
the forbidden implements. Out his fingertips flow
clouds of pure color flowering into feeling.
Slowly the veiled shapes reveal themselves.
Like a God looking down on the first world,
at Sëebull he sees shining upon the face of waters
the luminous oneness of all things,
paints his "Unpainted Pictures."

Kilometres away, across teal-blue marsh, grey sea,
daystars flash over Pëenemunde.

Hôtel du Rêve

At the dovecôte window
a huge eye glistens—moist
as a Blue Point oyster.
Through the unraveling sleeve
the dreamer's hand traces
across white spaces
a map of the night sky.
Over toy rooftops,
the glittering infinity
of mirrors & cities,
stars appear—Wanda Landowska,
Tamara Toumanova.

Trapped by his "wanderlust
nervousness," "the desparation
of trying to give shape to
obsession," the man in the cellar
picks his way among bric-a-brac,
tinsel detritus: glass beads,
bent bobbypins, old coins,
a shred of pink silk,
used jar of cold cream,
the electrolite lipstick case of
Hedy Lamarr, colored adverts for
Goldschmidt's fabulous
Mexican midgets &
dancing bears, DeMedici's
slot machine boy, three
Milky Way wrappers &
a fading snapshot of the Divine
Dietrich hailing a cab

outside the Apollo—all
the flotsam & jetsam of our lives
saved in a cigar box,
American Perfecto.

Held for a moment
in their second-hand glamour
& tender displacements
they glitter & shine.
"Voyager," they say,
"after centuries of nostalgia for the sea
(& the secrets of Empress Eugenie),
nothing is lost to the drift of time
or the intimate geography of memory.
Let the candle waver
before green light of landfall,
here you will find budding quince
& white wave breaking,
smell of wild mint, mown grass, gasoline,
even "the warm miracle,"
a snowball melting in a small boy's palm.
Look!
Shipwrecked against the Plaza's purple chateau,
the silver caravel of a cloud!"

Yes, it is 1942,
& there is a war going on.
From a Chicago basement,
where the chain reaction has begun,
word comes: *The Italian navigator*
                    has landed
               in the New World!
Flying through the window of the dream,
a crow explodes over Utopia Parkway.

Hôtel Mediterranée

"calme, luxe, et volupté"

What are you thinking about?
The earth? The sky? Our brief stay here? A good armchair?
The difference between things as the paint dries?
A hotel room is an island, an oasis, an ice-floe, a cube of light.
Inside, everything unfolds—flat, precise, cut out of time.
The flowers in a painted vase. The vase of painted flowers.
For the gentleman on the balcony
there is the luxury of watching smoke unfurl
its airy grillwork, lazy arabesques
over the harbor's rusted scow, the golden section of a sail,
electric tricolors rippling in the wind.
What thinks the thin king as he sinks into the fat lady's lap?
Ma mère, an early warning pearls the sky?
Back inside, a terra-cotta coffee urn,
ashtrayed Havana, smoldering rose,
the green paradise of pineapples on a plate
compose themselves before his gaze.
Like a stain on time, light dries.

I woke this morning from a buoyant dream,
a bare (left) nipple, pink bud, purple aureole
on which I suckled like a baby
while wave after wave the white blossoms of the stars
floated on the black lacquered surface of the sea
& a voice whispered to me, "Japanese snow."
Torso upright, he settles in his chair.
He watches what appears & reappears to him,
illusory patterns, lyric traceries,
shadows overflowing the bright shape
of ewer, pitcher, bowl,

a green line taking off the shine as plumbed
from his thumb the cut
of his blue suit rolls over into
lapels . . .

He bows before the contours of the hour.
He refuses to paint the scheduled flowers.
Behind him, mimicking the clock, a goldfish circles a bowl.
In the red studio, he says, everything is red.
therefore, black is the color of roses.
For those in a hurry let the avid Spanish monkey,
savage pansy, in his *penseés sauvage*
play with fire, disarrange the flames.
Churchbells. It is Sunday.
He dresses in his formal lawyer's suit to paint the nude.
He pays her double-overtime.
In this room where someone he does not know turns her back on
        him,
into the cold port & glassy harbor of his eye
hove to view
magenta swirl, canary flash
as the swelling fabric billowing to its fullest
swaying falls away before
the astonishing bodying forth of
what is there. Drawing in air,
the bald man with black spectacles & beard
exposes the frozen equations of repose,
archaic pose of elbows arching over corona of hair.
Along the undulating wall of light
mirrored by sea & sky like blinding semaphors
urgent pulsings, dazzled waverings—
rose delta brushed by blaze of white, invisible wings.

The Floating Studio

i

What does make you serious?
Pity for those who winter in numbers?
Restlessness that drives us beyond the city to the mountains,
    the sea?
Soyez mysterieuse of this room of white candles
where night after night the voluptuous ones wearily bloom
under the moon of too many mirrors?
Door to the river gulls mourn in mist,
women at an Arab funeral?
All day "beautiful & disconnected
as a waterlily" you float with the keeper of rivers,
who is always still, & see in the trembling lens
the pale faces of the brave dancing boys
drowned in the muddy trenches of France.
As the last star fades to *blanchisseries* of morning,
you write against all this whiteness,
"Love, death will paint you in flowers."

ii

The poem of undying love,
beautiful & embarrassing as a sunset in any language
has disappeared in pink foam, slippery egg-whites,
showers of gold. Where a cliché of swans
sails across black glass
someone has guillotined the tulips,
all the statues are bandaged & blind.

Silver shivers—schools of fish—flee
the shrapnelled wind that is
water running through the leaves
& you follow the sinuously unfolding cursives to
their final erasures,
the "too late, too late" of
"it never was," till the mystery of the way water flows
like the crazy answer to a crazy question
leads to the spectacle of a powerful hand
writing across a moving line of shadow
last words of a book which has no beginning
where it is still possible to imagine
a world of peasants without lords,
loving siestas behind drawn blinds,
"the coinless coin."

iii

While it is easy to dispell these windows
as mirrors in another language
the linguistic error abides—in the city of cygnes
the education of the heart never ends,
& though you carry your hunch charmingly
the arrival in stages has led us to a Palace of Steam
rising above the dream of rivers
where these marmoreal sleepers in their snowy repose
seem about to wake out of seafoam rock
or slowly sink back into it.
Beneath the colored portico,
the bearded god of willow banks
reclines between two nymphs who offer in shallow red bowls
the pellucid blue of perpetual noon.

i v

"Yesterday,
I was married under the chestnut trees
to a passing shadow
by the sun.
            Then the bees started swarming,
& everything fell apart.
                        Today, it is raining,
& it is not raining—the opaque transparency
of floating islands—wild colors
daubed on glass.
                        Ah, the patois of goats
& coconuts, these flags plea-bargaining with the wind.
                        Darling,
                                    is this the joy
whose garment is sorrow?
I am tired of closing the eyes of the dead."

v

What do you desire?
The refrain that will not repeat itself?
A dove windowed in flight—pane after pane after pane?
Beyond the tyranny of naming & framing
we see the invisible job of creation &
all the animals with numbers in their heads.
As always we are surprised by
the astonishing news our bodies bring us—intelligence
from afar—& as the stars lose their influence
& blackbirds steal fire from the sky
what closes over us—with a hint

of menace—is a violent illumination
of the barbed wire text.

v i

On the other side of the river of moving mirrors
brilliant talkers who bring down the night
are feeding hallucinogens to the pigeons.
As only the chaste can inflame,
ashes speak to us, saying,
"You have been given the gift of time
that, in time, you may renounce it."
O, my sister,
where in all our wandering shall we find
another to love us,
to love?

Black Suit

Forget the great bloodlettings of history.
The shape of the enigma reveals what it is hiding.
At night the teeth float in your face, a shark in dark waters.
As the prow pulls away from the pier, you wave good-bye to
    the baby.
Waking you say, "Yes, the mountains *are* mountains.
The men are all well-dressed & none of them are women.
But that was long ago & luck is not our long suit.
Here, when the beloved dies, we strangle a stranger.
& when we become too transparent to ourselves?"
Unrolling the rug in the dream you discover
how pain translates into sexual pleasure,
gold keyhole, iron horseshoe, sizzle of salted oysters on ice.
"Art begins in a wound," she says,
"like the death of one we love better than ourselves,
like heartsickness, homesickness, psychic lightning,
like, *I am dancing with cancer.*"
Still, the stone does its work day & night.
We gaze & gaze across the waters
but cannot tell who sails in the boat approaching.

Sisyphus of Birds,
may we dine forever at the Table of Breath
so dense & so serene with angels.
Verdant hills await us, marble slabs above a landlocked sea,
beds of clamshells shimmering with feathers, iridescent
    mirrored doves.
Your Lucky Numbers are 33,38,43,44,45,47

All the warning signs are here & news of the late arrivals,
slow & elegant as scarves of winter smoke—

mirrorwalkers, pushpin terrorists,
bored metaphysicians of oysters & angels,
midnight tricksters who stole the master's tools.
Here is scary authority & the double arrogance of power,
the virtual hand in hyperspace.
A steel wind cuts the throat of dawn—
red upsilon, wishbone vibrato,
& the Dance of Utter Darkness begins.
Holding the hideous purple blooms, they sing:

Black suit, black suit, my invisible one,
Black suit, black suit, you have swallowed the sun's gold rays!
Black suit, black suit, black as the blackest King of Crows,
Black as the palest cabby's shadow,
Give up the ghost, black suit, black suit.
Black suit, black suit, you are dying.
The rose was once the earth, black suit,
A five-pointed star plucked from a madman's eye!

iv

Cygnus Olor

Who is as lonely as we are?
An eskimo on an ice-floe under the blue Arctic sun
pities us, who have forgotten death
& invented the loveless lie of one life only,
elephants by firefly light. Love, this death is a noise
that never stops, I hear it everywhere—
a hairsbreadth out of sight—turning blessings
into curses, like spitting in cold soup,
& though they say, "It's alright, it's alright,"
somehow I know it isn't—all our gaiety
chirping of a smoke alarm before the battery dies.
Just yesterday I noticed tips of birches
reddening—the slow meltdown
to spring—felt a sudden fear
for all things that grow in the radiant half-life
of the Shadow—Three Mile Island's
monstrous ferns, colorless flowers of Chernobyl.
Now, as the Apostle of the Waves
gathers all his keys together
for the final loss, light years away,
Dark Star, your silence sings to me
all the things I dare not say. Shape of absence, echo
without word, you are the negative
by which we live, kiss of space
that speeds us on our way . . .

Pays-Bas

There is a pain you cannot know & a life
displayed like "The Classic Map of the World,"
its primary colors, countries—Leeuwenhoek's "animalcules"
aswim in the magnifying glass of the moon,
& continents—massive amoeba drifting
the blue culture of seas. Weary of the narrative line,
you surrender to the split-second seductions
of the pure impressional as though the eye's glassy globe
were all, the perfect gesture flung to completion, a wave
moving in stillness, firelight flowing
ricepaper shades—this succession of cities
shelving to the sea. Outside diamond-dark Antwerp,
smell of dung & hydrangea; greenhouses lit by tulip-bulb glow;
jutting Rotterdam's oozy weir of poles & powerlines,
the atomic plant—a giant milk churn.
As land gives way to watery prairies, maritime plains,
windmills center a luminous sky
slanting North light navigates—pearl-grey, rose-cobalt
cloud-archipelagoes. Here, locks lift almost to eye-level
a schooner's firelily sail, the yellow barge
where an oil-slickered captain stands,
dreaming the big dredgers of Jakarta.
Crisscrossing watermirroringsky,
snowy egret, guillemot, spoonbill, gull—whiteoutriders
of the moving shadow, flocks of marsh harrier
back from ancient mossy-stoned North Sea dikes,
in their throats silver mackerel
to feed the fiercely hungering young,
a black Bedouin army oasised in chalk & alkali islands
under the wavering Nordic sun.
Slowly the signs detach themselves—*vit-vaart, rekening.*

The eye scans dark stars—smashed factory windows,
verdigris poignancy of the first pissoir,
chimney-brick dusk, red cabbage steaming coal ovens,
this fragile network of canals & bridges
reclaimed—like Faust's last great task—from the sea,
Amsterdam, city of reflections & flowers.
Here the day's shrewd business & holy obligations
banked in good faith, shameful secrets
whispered on Sabbath to the Father of Lies.
Spare white geometry of rooms, curtainless windows—
the Dutch interior—fumed oak, polished teak, blue tiles,
harbormaster's clock & *waterkaart* on wall,
somber lamp blooming in a Delft vase,
& the limpid & gentle spring of the Gospels flowing
from the minister's posthumous son,
beside him, the brown-shawled widow, his mother, knitting,
        knitting.

Gît-le-Coeur

Twenty-one years later return—
shadowy Alley of Nightingales,
dove-grey shutters, rouged chimney pots, tiles,
slow explosions of flowers on scrollwork,
rainslick paving stones that reflect
Plato's beautiful phrase,
"the other side of the sky"—
Street-Where-the-Heart-Lies.

In the Hotel of Last Light they stand:
blue-haloed Madame Rachoud;
her window-cat, Myrto;
Arlette, the hooker, whose yellow cockatiel
whistled *La Marseillaise* at the bar;
axman Lorenzo, blinded by black ice;
sweet Ali, the hashish-seller, sipping mint tea;
Texas junkie Rose, her grey benedictions;
the Dutchman who banished *six*
from the dictionary;
ibis-eyed Nazli, whirling
in a scarf of smoke & flame;
& above them all, Doctor Seraphicus
whose black magic lit
the tulips of Luxembourg
the night you saw the tiger-sky,
heard ten thousand monkeys
chattering in a cloud.
Drifting under this glass roof,
you listened to the city breathing,
its hypnotic ebb & flow
broken by the dark staccato—

plastique, gunfire in the streets.
Morning, curfew lifted,
blue-uniformed Senegalese
fished new bodies from the Seine.

Twenty-one years later,
crossing the river again,
9 *Gît-le-Coeur* has become
the three-star *Aux Vieux Paris.*
The bored nightclerk, reciting
Notre-Dame des Fleurs to his lover,
exchanges an iron key
for your passport & your name.
Upstairs, someone is singing
"Red River Valley."
Lying alone in this small bed
you feel the perfumed evening flower
from sour sheets & sweating pores,
the slowly threshing fan that throws
fantastic shadows on ceiling & on wall,
gold *L* of door & lintel where
darkness begins whispering,

> *Traveler, you have come so far*
> *only to arrive in time*
> *& where you are.*
> *Here you may have*
> *all you fear & desire.*
> *What do you desire?*

Vigil

In another life, I would have chosen you above all others—your
        lustrous darks, shy disquietudes.
Where ghosts of birds skim the wired air, I sit before moon-
        blankened paper & stare
At the future's shrouded tables, mirrors, chairs. Below the
        landlord's octagonal tower & cedar-shingled stables
Sleekfinned limousines ripple liquid darkness toward
        Stillwater Road. Beyond the harbor gates
I hear the baffled horn & suddenly I am lost again, counting
        rabbits in the fog.

My bride of unrequited brightness, in our rented paradise where
        the homely mysteries bloom—labor & love,
A kitchen's white hive, morning glories flowering over a
        cast iron black & gold 40s Chambers stove,
"The infinity stone," doorstop from the sea, what is it troubles
        me? Last night's broken dream?
The Mystic Writing Pad of Sleep lifted like a magic slate
        erasing what is brought to light?
Vigil of white roses? Breath of invisible horses in the mist?

What was it woke me? Muffled footsteps? Freakish heat
        lightning? Tinny transparency of prayer bells
Shivering in the wind? That thin shadow at the door? Startled
        out of sleep, I smelled stale sweat & ozone,
Heard as though in the next stall the cry of a small child,
        weeping, weeping—echo of forgotten heartbreak,
Aftershock & ache of some ancient pain I no longer feel, but
        own, & owning am once more at home
In this strange place again, its cedar shingles lavendered by
        rain.

Swan

Putting down the pen,
you stare at *aster*,
isolate & sad,
seeing as though for the last time
in the fading lessness
of the word an icy omen
windowing a world.
Book of Breath,
pale star,
what is sayable, to be said?
Was it only yesterday
walking back uphill
hand in hand with a child
you heard the woman tell
the story of sleep
no one ever wakens from,
dark winter light's
zero degree
melting on that salt shore
where the sea gives up
its frigid green mysteries
& on a bed of straw
like frozen foam
saw the pure curve &
inviolate whiteness of
that all-but-breathing
fallen form
whose still warm wing
offered you this feather
to write the dream of wild horses?

Tierra del Uomo

The white rush was the shadow of what wounds you.
& though the melodies are often different
& sometimes the meanings
the object is always the same.
Evening star, morning star,
an overall husbandry of means prevails,
seeing how far we can go
on how little,
the crowsnest theory of perfect fires
which, when we wish each other well,
takes us to the common place where we discover
what we look for is what we find,
that dry country where they trap in pools sudden rain.
What moves us now beyond ourselves
touches us with these distant feelings as
before the storm,
lento, lento, we hear
the terrible horses stamping in their stalls.
A circus of birds chatters above still waters.
& although he arrives before you,
you recognize the stranger.
As you wipe steam from the window,
you see his black hat among white roses of smoke,
waving, slowly waving.

Writing in the Rain

Always we come up against the illusory net with real holes,
someone's idea of a wall.
Still, the white flock *is* the paper.
When all fly away but one, *that* is the nightbird.
Flushed from morning fields,
what spoke to you was the ghost of love in a Japanese movie,
frottage of feelings, out-takes of the dream.
Now the black taxi glides to the curb.
Through bluesmoked windows you see,
like a memory of the future,
the one who whispers, "Yes, I have a friend in the city."

In the Place of the Absence of Desire

The white map of the river led us to
what I took to be flames in a furnace,
you, doves over a winter sea.

You said, *I have just come back*
from the far side of the moon,
nothing, nothing, can ever be the same.

In the rushing blackness
of the subway home, we sat face to face.
I said, *You tell me where we're going,*
I'll tell you where we've been . . .

Where are you now, old friend?
How many winters have passed into spring?

Black Spring

            The least thing
calls you back to me—blue naiads
by a stream, day lilies straining
toward first light, the dark allegory
of the lake swarming with stars.
In a flash I see you risen—
my sore rose Eros—ecstatic
in the mounting flush, a volcano
under snow, crowing to greet
the dawn within you.
                    Darkness
dazzles, mothwings shadowing
a flame, & I feel the pain—
the moving picture of our lives
now glossy stills, a foreign city
after rain.
                At the bay window where,
binoculars in hand, I named
all the birds from the book
you gave me, piloting us to
the eye of the storm, breathing deep,
I let myself relax into
the inevitable unfolding of light.
Slowly, my old friend the mountain
is revealed to me, luminous
in its mantle of mist, then ragged lines
of needlepoint pine, meadows overflowing
clover, vetch where the sorrel mare
once swam, & shining shining
in a shaken sea of apples,
the barn's dark ark.

                    As shade by shade
night's black lilac, greying,
fades, gathering in its going
a memory of color that once
was love, I see you swept away—
pale ocean bird, hanging, an instant,
outspread between the wave's white veil,
angelus of the morning star.

Blue Flower

Sailing always against the prevailing
you have come to the fever chart's
red archipelagoes,
that low country where
rivers mourn the memory of a sky.
Daily friends bring you
green turtle shells from the Cape Verde Islands,
Peruvian lilies, the leper stone
that appears in the ocean
when Venus is on the Western horizon,
miraculous cures of the Virgin of Snows.
Floating on eggshells you hear
the lady electricians
in their long skirts of wind, of rain
whispering as they pass by,
Scissors . . . Knives . . .
At the icy interior of your fear
an angry mole, blind pioneer
burrows upward cell by cell
toward shivering spires,
steeples of starlight.
What is illness, then?
A heavenly mode of locomotion?
This melody that has its teeth in you?
The dark side of how the stars shine?
Ah, you are tired of your mind,
the "here" that is always "elsewhere,"
& as shockwaves break
against the pure impossibility of this loss,
the rock of the body,
you know the wall is real

& reality the final illusion.
Waking now to fever, chills,
fog in your bones,
the first bird singing on the pale branch of morning,
light is too painful.
Close your eyes.
You feel the buried thunder of the pulse,
whole worlds suspended in a honeyed drop,
the unbearable weight of the bee on the blossom,
& on the blank tablet write
in a hand not quite your own
Forge . . . Forgetfulness . . .
as though this were the only life there is.

Island

"The first breath," she says,
"shall take you back to childhood."
& the second breath . . . ?

Always to come back to
this deep place where someone
is breathing you—gills of white light, rosebush on water.

Listen.
The wind is sharpening its knives.
Someone is turning the pages of the sea.

Kicking, swim
to the window where
two statues embrace in falling snow.
She who holds the night in her arms
looks down at you smiling.
"This is your father home on furlough."

O, great white bell of memory melting . . .
Out of the cloud factory come
the women in their skirts of evergreen
gathering from the foaming shore
Lithuania's electric honey, amber of invisible bees.

All night the dark shapes circle overhead,
blankly black & shining, shining.
"Every day's an alibi," they say.
"Even Nothing has a mother."
A quicksilver stick strikes the blind sky
& someone cries, "The red rooster is loose!"
Gloved hands lift you toward a giant horse on ice.

Here is the gold napkin ring
engraved with your birthdate & a stranger's name.
The shipwrecked wing,
sea of shattered glass, fiery islands of debris,
the black motorcycle spinning in space.
Here is blood & milk,
alluvial murmurs of a moon,
the single white stone no one atones for.

Who rescues you?
A boy with small ears
whose name contains the mother-of-waters.
Watcher over milkcans in a kosher dairy,
she wraps you in her shawl of grey roses,
looks death in the eye, & laughs,
"I've seen a bigger dwarf!"

How old is the wind?
Does the salt miller weep for the sea?
Ah, little one, let the sky write itself.
Close your eyes. Blow the candle out.
Now, breathe deeply, after me . . .

Talking to the Ancestors

Easter
of invisible sailing—wing
of the swan—you want to get back to
silence before the first word is spoken
& the black horse drinks from the lily of light,
'til someone says in a language that finally makes sense
  to us,
I'm blind, give me an eel, I'll eat it,
give me a snake, I'll eat it,
& the man who plays with his eye on the Beast
lifts the diamond from your heart,
all the dark obsequies & beautiful lies
the night tells itself
so it can sleep,
& the stars flow back to us, burning, burning, upon the
  black lake.

Notes

"Loom" quotes at the end a letter from George Oppen who, in his final days, suffered from Alzheimer's.

"Muntzer" uses images from the sermons and speeches of Thomas Muntzer, the fiery German social reformer and mystic Anabaptist pastor executed for his role in the peasant revolts of 1524-25.

"Reading after Dark" was occasioned by a lecture on Ruskin by Robert Harbison.

"Hôtel du Rêve" draws from the selected diaries, letters and files edited by Mary Ann Caws in *Joseph Cornell's Theater of the Mind*. The phrase "green light of landfall" comes from the journals of Christopher Columbus. *"The Italian navigator has landed in the New World!"* was the coded message announcing the creation of an atomic chain reaction by Enrico Fermi.

"Hotel Mediterranée" is indebted to the essays on Henri Matisse by William S. Wilson.

"Black Suit" derives its last lines from writings quoted in Anne Hollander's *Sex and Suits: The Evolution of Modern Dress*. *"We gaze and gaze across the waters . . ."* is taken from David Ferry's rendering into English verse of *Gilgamesh*.

"Cygnus Olor" is the "mute swan" who sings only at its death. Informing the poem also is *Cygnus X-1*, a dark star or black hole "sighted" in the Northern Cross.